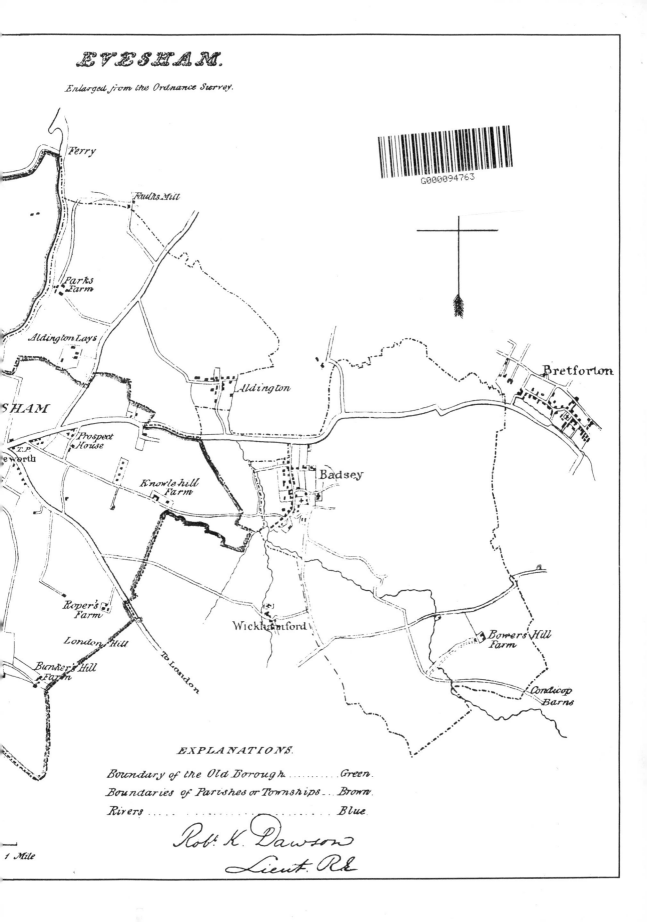

EVESHAM.

Enlarged from the Ordnance Survey.

G000094763

Ferry

Faulks Mill

Parks Farm

Aldington Lays

SHAM

Aldington

Bretforton

Prospect House

T.P.
eworth

Knowle hill Farm

Badsey

Roper's Farm

London Hill

Wickhamford

Bowers Hill Farm

Bunker's Hill Farm

To London

Condicop Barns

EXPLANATIONS.

Boundary of the Old Borough . . . . Green.

Boundaries of Parishes or Townships . . . Brown.

Rivers . . . . Blue.

Robt. K. Dawson

Lieut. R.E.

1 Mile

EVESHAM
A Pictorial History

The Bell Tower by E. H. New.

EVESHAM
A Pictorial History

Arthur H. Fryer
and
Josephine Jeremiah

Phillimore

1994

Published by
PHILLIMORE & CO. LTD.,
Shopwyke Manor Barn, Chichester, West Sussex

ISBN 0 85033 935 9

Printed and bound in Great Britain by
BIDDLES LTD.
Guildford, Surrey

List of Illustrations

Frontispiece: The Bell Tower

Churches and Chapels

The Town

The River

Acknowledgements

We have made every effort to establish copyright where possible and obtain permission to reproduce, but if we have inadvertently omitted any names we apologise. Our thanks go to the following institutions and individuals for their help in enabling us to compile this selection:

Almonry Museum, Evesham, Mr. G. Barnett, Bookworms of Evesham, Lt. Col. R.G. Burlingham, Mr. N. Cole, Dr. D. Cox B.A. Ph.D. F.S.A., Mrs. C. Evans, Evesham Library, Mr. D. Fryer, Mr. Reg Gould, Mr. R. Hart, Mrs. J.P. Hemming, Mr. P. Hemming, Mr. M. Heritage, Journal Series, Evesham, (formerly W. and H. Smith), Mr. A. Knott, Mr. T. Malin, Mrs. D. Green, Miss I. Masters, Mr. R. Newbury, Mrs. B. O'Connor, Mr. D. Witts.

We would particularly like to thank Mrs. Phyllis Fryer and Mr. Ian Jeremiah for their research and help in selecting material for this book.

The map is reproduced from the (1831) Ordnance Survey (2 in. to 1 mile) map with the permission of the Controller of H.M.S.O.

Introduction

Evesham is the centre of the Vale which extends from the foot of the Cotswolds to Bredon Hill in the south west and the rising ground of the Lenches in the north. There is considerable evidence as to its earliest inhabitants. During the Palaeolithic period, 40,000-75,000 years ago, Mousterian men were in the area. Stone tools used by them have been found on Bredon Hill. Occasionally discoveries are made of stone implements from the period 6,000-8,000 years ago when Britain was separated from Europe by the submergence of land now underneath the English Channel. When this happened the tribes left behind moved to the higher grounds such as the Cotswolds, Bredon Hill and the ridge of the Lenches. These people were later overrun by Neolithic tribes from Europe.

Finds of pottery in Broadway and the discovery of an axe at Badsey tell us that Neolithic men were followed by Bronze Age men who worked in the Vale somewhere between 1,800-1,500 B.C. Iron Age men were in the district from about 500 B.C. and coins from this pre-Roman era have turned up around Bredon Hill. The Romans arrived in Britain around A.D. 43 and, noting the Vale as a fertile area for growing food, they occupied the land cleared of forest to feed their armies and the civilians who accompanied them. Much evidence of their occupation has been found along the banks and tributaries of the River Avon in places such as Badsey and Aldington. Earthenware fragments and coins have been uncovered in Hampton at Gypsies' Corner and Peewit Lane, but very few artefacts on the site of Evesham itself.

Christianity, introduced by the Romans, still flourished after they left in the early 5th century. There were isolated areas of Saxons by the 6th century but Evesham was always on the extreme edge of Saxon administration. When, in 577, the Saxons defeated British leaders at Dyrham, in Gloucestershire, the Vale of Evesham was taken over first by Wessex and later by Mercia. Pagan burial grounds from this period have been found at Broadway, Beckford and Fairfield in Evesham. After the death in 654 of Penda, king of Mercia, Christianity began to spread under the influence of his sons Peada, Wulfhere and Ethelred. Evesham was in the great diocese of Lichfield but under Ethelred it became part of the see of Worcester. This rise in Christianity laid the foundations of Evesham.

The uninhabited area which became Evesham was high ground in a loop of the River Avon. It was well-wooded, being the southern end of the royal forest of Feckenham where the bishops of Worcester were allowed to run their pigs. Legend says that Eoves, the swineherd of Ecgwin, Bishop of Worcester, was looking for lost pigs in the forest when he saw a vision of the Virgin Mary accompanied by two angels. Hurrying to his master, Eoves told him what he had seen and when the bishop came to the spot to find out for himself, he, too, beheld the same vision. It is said that Ecgwin then decided this was a sign that he must build an abbey to the glory of the Virgin Mary on the site.

However, it is more likely, as William of Malmesbury writing in the 12th century suggests, that there had been a small Saxon church at this location and because it was such a fertile area with an equitable climate Ecgwin was persuaded to resign as bishop of Worcester and to build an abbey at Evesham. Whatever the truth of these accounts, the foundation of the abbey was the beginning of the town which was named Eoveshomme, after the swineherd. In 701 Ethelred, by royal charter, conferred on Ecgwin the lands of Evesham, also endowing the abbey with a fort at Chadbury and a monastic community at Fladbury. A fuller charter in 709 endowed the abbey with 60 manses or farms on both sides of the River Avon. The abbey was dedicated to the Virgin Mary by Wilfred, Bishop of Worcester in 714 and Ecgwin was confirmed as its first abbot.

Ecgwin features in another tale concerning Evesham which has been handed down through the centuries. The legend goes that, when he was bishop of Worcester, malicious stories were spread about him which resulted in the bishop making a visit to the Pope in Rome to clear his name. Ecgwin wanted to demonstrate that his innocence could triumph over difficulties, so he resolved to walk to the papal city with his ankles shackled together. Having locked the fetters together the key was thrown into the river at Evesham. The bishop, upon his arrival in Rome, instructed one of his servants to catch a fish in the Tiber for the next meal. The outcome of this was that on cutting open the fish the very key which had been cast into the Avon at Evesham was revealed! Ecgwin was acquitted of all the accusations by the Pope and the shackles and chain were symbolised on the arms of Evesham Abbey.

Ecgwin's church had fallen down in 960 and a replacement built. This in turn was followed by a grander building which was consecrated in 1054 during the abbacy of Abbot Mannig. Walter, the first Norman abbot, commenced the construction of an even greater abbey church. Succeeding abbots continued with this work and throughout the medieval period Evesham Abbey grew in splendour. As the numbers of brethren increased so did the conventual buildings which became more and more well-appointed. Shortly after 1160 when Evesham Abbey became a mitred abbey, with papal authority for the wearing of mitres by its abbots, it ranked among the greatest monastic establishments in the country.

1265 saw the Battle of Evesham. Simon de Montfort, Earl of Leicester, who was married to Henry III's sister, led the barons of England against the king and his eldest son, the Lord Edward. Defeating Henry at Lewes, he marched to Evesham. Yet, although he was reputed to be a brilliant leader, on arrival he neglected to post guards on the only route out of the town which did not cross the river. Meanwhile, the Lord Edward had marched overnight from Kenilworth and in the morning had the bridge covered and his main troops in position across the top of Greenhill. This effectively cut off any escape for de Montfort's army. They were slaughtered and de Montfort was killed and cut into pieces. The battle was short and swift and the rising quashed.

The legend of Eoves had brought large numbers of pilgrims to the abbey but after de Montfort's death there was a great upsurge of pilgrims coming to the Vale. Miraculous cures were claimed after visits to the spring known as Battlewell, situated at the top of Greenhill. This spring also came to be called the Earl's Well or the Martyr's Fountain. The town had to expand to accommodate these pilgrims. Many extra houses were built, some encroaching upon the abbey precincts, with the result that the abbot ordered them to be pulled down. An abbey wall was erected to prevent this occurring again.

In 1327 Edward III granted letters patent to the bailiffs and good men of Evesham who were given authority to levy tolls on goods entering the town. This increase in business life gave the abbots more money to spend on the abbey. Each succeeding abbot improved and added new buildings. Clement Lichfield, the last real abbot, erected the magnificent Bell

Tower which is still standing to this day. It was finished in 1538, two years before the dissolution of the abbey.

When Henry VIII sent his men into Evesham Abbey in 1540, Abbot Lichfield, rather than hand over his beloved abbey, retired to the manor of Offenham, a sick man. In his place Philip Hawford, a monk whose family name was Ballard, was appointed abbot. His job was to surrender the abbey without causing problems for the king, his reward being a yearly pension of £240 and permission to live in the almonry. The rest of the monks were turned out with a pension of £3 per annum.

At the dissolution the king offered the abbey to the people of Evesham for £300, but to the detriment of the town the offer was declined and Sir Philip Hoby bought it, as well as a portion of the abbey lands. The abbey was quickly pulled down and the stone and timbers sold off for building material. A large part of the Town Hall, built by Sir Philip Hoby, is of abbey stone, while pieces of it were found recently when the Cheltenham & Gloucester Building Society renovated their building in Bridge Street. The almonry was left standing and is now the town museum, housing an impressive selection of artefacts from the abbey and the town, the great abbot's chair and the quarter boys from the Bell Tower, the abbey bible with a hand-written account by one of the monks of the dissolution as it happened and many more treasures.

For a time after the dissolution Evesham was somewhat depressed as the people were used to the strong leadership of the abbey and being sustained when sick and poor by the almoner. Now they were required to do these things for themselves. However, gradually trading resumed and again Evesham began to thrive. Dr. Lewis Bayley, the minister of All Saints Church (1600-11) and chaplain to James I's eldest son, Prince Henry, influenced the latter to persuade his father to grant Evesham a charter in 1603, which gave the town borough status. A second charter was granted in 1605, incorporating Bengeworth, the village across the river. The holding of three fairs each year was permitted by the 1605 charter, plus two markets every week on Mondays and Fridays. By 1636 Evesham had become one of the nine highest-rated corporate towns in England, after the cities and county towns, being required to pay £74 in 'ship money', the tax imposed by Charles I.

It was in 1636 that William Sandys of Fladbury started constructing locks and sluices on the River Avon. By 1639, at a cost of between £20,000 and £40,000, the river became navigable for the 43 miles between Tewkesbury and Stratford. Towed by gangs of strong men, the early barges bore large square sails and were about 35ft. long. They carried a variety of goods. Opening the river for trade was very much to Evesham's benefit especially as the river barges brought fuel to the town, a commodity which was scarce in the Vale.

Not long after the opening of the navigation came the Civil War. Evesham became involved in the conflict because it was situated on the direct route from Oxford to Wales. Charles I held court here from 4 July to 13 July 1644 at a house in Bridge Street known as Langstone's House. Evesham had never been a fortified town, the main entrance being over the bridge linking Bengeworth and Evesham. When the king and his troops moved out, having broken down the bridge, the Parliamentarians under Sir William Waller advanced on the town. Returning to Evesham, the king fined the town £200 for repairing the bridge and allowing Waller to enter.

During the Protectorate of Oliver Cromwell most sections of the church in Evesham were given religious freedom, except for the Society of Friends. Known as Quakers, they commenced their meetings in 1655 at the house of Thomas Cartwright, a glover, which was probably in Port Street. Much abuse was encountered, the Rev. George Hopkins, vicar of

All Saints and an avowed Presbyterian, leading the persecution. Friends were imprisoned for refusing to take the oath of abjuration and more than 60 Quaker books were burnt at the market cross. A purpose-built meeting house was erected in Cowl Street in 1676 which is still standing to this day. Most of the early Friends were business people and they lie in the burial ground at the rear of the building. Edward Pitway, a mayor of Evesham, belonged to the sect but was removed from the Council when he joined the Society of Friends.

The Baptists first met in a private house, building in 1704 a small meeting house in Bengeworth which was replaced by another in 1722. Burnt down by a fire in Port Street in 1759, this was soon rebuilt. The big chapel in Cowl Street was finished in 1788 and there has always been an active church there. It was substantially altered in 1979, the old school room being demolished and a complex of retirement flats built around it.

The Presbyterians, later known as the Unitarians, started meeting in a barn on the west side of High Street. The present chapel was built in Oat Street in 1737. Many eminent local townspeople worshipped there including George May, the New family and the Gill Smith family. In later times Mrs. Amy Nightingale, headmistress of the Infants' Council School in the 1920s and the first woman to be mayor of Evesham, was a prominent member.

Methodism came to Evesham later, but thanks to the many visits paid by John and Charles Wesley to the area, when they stayed with the headmaster of the Deacle School, it grew rapidly in strength and was extremely well-organised, becoming the strongest of the nonconformist groups. Their first church was in use by 1808, built on the site of what was the Council School in Swan Lane. The present church at the bottom of Bridge Street by the Workman Bridge was opened in 1907. This was extensively renovated in 1979 when the Sunday School rooms were sold and the money used to modernise the church, which has a thriving congregation to this day.

Other religious denominations exist in the town including The Salvation Army, well-known for their good work among the elderly and poor. Their hall was badly damaged in 1977 when the adjacent factory caught fire. New premises were opened in The Leys in 1989.

Catholics in Evesham at one time worshipped in a corrugated iron church in Magpie Lane, now called Avon Street, which was opened in 1887. In 1907 the official marriage ceremony between Princess Louise d'Orleans and Prince Charles de Bourbon-Siciles was solemnised there. The building of the new St Mary's Catholic church, in High Street, was finished in 1912.

Evesham is unusual in having two parish churches in the same churchyard. They are All Saints, which in the pre-Reformation period was the church of the people and St Lawrence, now redundant, which was the church of the pilgrims. Joining the two parishes with a footing in each one is the abbey's Bell Tower. There are other Anglican churches at Bengeworth and Hampton. The church of St Peter at Bengeworth replaced a medieval building in Church Street, pulled down in 1870. Several items were taken from the old church and installed in the new one, the John Deacle memorial being among them. The Burlingham family who lived in Lansdowne House, opposite the church, paid for the clock tower to be built. St Andrew's, the parish church at Hampton, has a record of vicars who have served there since the 8th century but little is known of the early church buildings used by the priests and their congregations. Some pieces of Norman moulding are built into the nave of the church, having probably been incorporated when it was reconstructed in 1282. The church was enlarged in the 15th century and has hardly changed since that time.

The education of children in Evesham was initially connected with the abbey church. From the reign of Edward III schooling for boys had been provided within Evesham Abbey.

During the abbacy of Clement Lichfield a school was erected on nearby Merstow Green, an open space belonging to the town, but this closed at the dissolution of the abbey. Now part of the Working Men's Club, the porch of this building still stands with the abbey arms over the door. The boys' school recommenced under the 1605 charter and was called 'The Free Grammar School of Prince Henry in Evesham'. It survived, with several interruptions, until 1879 when it was transferred to a building on Greenhill. The school carried on there until 1911 when new premises were built at the end of Victoria Avenue. It has remained in this location ever since with numerous additions and changes in status.

There was only private education for girls until the 1780s when the Sunday School movement was started to provide education for those children not receiving any form of instruction. In 1805 the Rev. Samuel Field established a Sunday school in the town hall. From this stemmed the National School, which the National Society, founded by the Church of England, opened in Evesham in 1812. It was moved for a time into the grammar school premises on Merstow Green but when it fell into disorder plans were made to set up the grammar school again. In 1831 a new National School was erected on Merstow Green with a larger establishment following in 1844. The latter has now been replaced by St Richard's C. of E. First School, built in 1986 on the Four Pools estate.

Education at the National School in Evesham was not provided for children with non-conformist backgrounds so in 1845 a school was built in Swan Lane for these children, this property later being used as a Masonic Hall. In 1846 a British School was set up at the top of Conduit Hill which carried on until 1869. This establishment, after reconstruction, eventually became Evesham County Primary School and then Swan Lane First School. The premises were in use until 1990 when a new school was built in The Rynal. Now the old school houses County Council offices.

In the mid 17th century Bengeworth children were taught to read and write by the Rev. Henry Wilson who used St Catherine's Chapel in the old church for this purpose until about 1654, when he was ousted by the Puritans. John Deacle, a native of Bengeworth, who had made a great deal of money in London as a woollen draper, left provision in his will of 1706 to help 30 of the poorest boys in the parish to be educated and apprenticed. A clause in the will stated, 'that the children be carefully taught and that the schoolmaster may wholly apply himself to their instruction; that no person in ecclesiastical orders whatsoever shall be admitted to fill that situation'. The master appointed received a salary of £20 per annum but later this was augmented to £30. An example of the distinctive uniform, which was a 'vest of blue kersey woollen cloth, with petticoat of yellow cloth and one blue cap', can be seen in the Almonry Museum. When the Deacle School closed around 1906 its endowments were combined with those of Prince Henry's Grammar School.

Bengeworth's girls were not educated unless their parents could afford private schooling. This was rectified when a National School was established near the old church in 1841. It was in existence until 1896 when a new National School was built on the corner of Kings Road and Lime Street to provide places for the increasing number of children in the district. Known in later years as Bengeworth C.E. First School, this in turn has been replaced by a new school in Burford Road which was built in 1991.

The growth of Evesham has necessitated the building of a number of new schools, four having been erected in close proximity on the Four Pools estate. These are Evesham High School, Vale of Evesham School, Simon de Montfort Middle School and St Richard's C. of E. First School. St Andrew's C.E. First School at Hampton has modern classrooms as does St Egwin's C.E. Middle School. Other schools in Evesham include St. Mary's R.C.

Primary School and the private school on Greenhill which is located in the premises of the former grammar school before its move to Victoria Avenue.

The population of Evesham has continued to rise steadily since records began. In 1801 the figure was 2,837 and this had increased to 4,245 by 1841. At the turn of the century in 1901 the population stood at 7,101 but by mid-century in 1951 it had climbed to 12,062. Evesham's residents now total approximately 18,000.

The trades that past inhabitants of Evesham followed were diverse. In late medieval times people were engaged in the cottage industries of making woollen cloth, caps and garments. During the monastic period there were fullers in Bengeworth who fulled cloth for the monks' habits. Also in Bengeworth were glovers making sheep-skin and dog-skin gloves. At the time of the Civil War Evesham was required to provide 1,000 pairs of boots for the Royalist soldiers. This indicates that shoe-making was an important industry in the town. By the 18th century many people were involved in the making of leather goods and the industry was at its height by the middle of the century. A wide range of trades and businesses also flourished. Thomas Mann set up silk throwstering in the 1770s and this occupation was carried on by others, including Anthony Stratton. Begun during monastic times, parchment-making in Bengeworth survived until the close of the 19th century under the direction of the Tipper family who supplied law firms and the War Office with their product. Nail-making, another Bengeworth trade, lasted until the early years of the 20th century and was conducted in Nailers' Row, where horse-nails were forged; cart-nails, used for securing sectional tyres to farmers' wagons and carts, being made further down The Leys. The nails were carried down to the river in baskets to be sent on barges to Gloucester.

During the 18th century as businesses expanded so did trade on the river. By 1751, when an act of Parliament fixed the rates of tonnage and tolls, commerce along the navigation had increased so much that about 400 craft were plying for trade on the Avon. George May, in his *Descriptive history of the town of Evesham*, published in 1845, mentioned that the 'convenient quays and wharfs near Evesham bridge also afford commodious landing and warehouse-room for goods of every description'. These substantial wharves comprised a public wharf, six private wharves and two timber yards. They were used for unloading imports such as coal, sugar, iron and wood, and for loading local merchandise which included corn, cheese, boots and shoes and garden crops.

The Vale of Evesham is justly famous for its fruit-growing and market gardening. While some may believe that this industry was begun during the monastic period, according to T.R. Nash in his *Collections for the history of Worcestershire* (1781) an Italian Francis Bernardi, the son of a Genoese ambassador, was the inspiration for horticulture in the Vale and is reputed to have spent a great deal in developing the science of growing in Evesham.

As London expanded, nurserymen from Middlesex sold their land for development and moved away, a number of them coming to the Vale of Evesham and to Offenham, in particular. Here James Myatt settled and started experimenting with crops other than the cereals for which the Vale had always been renowned. Cabbages, sprouts and leeks were introduced and he began improving the varieties to suit the land. To this day Myatt's early Offenham cabbage is still grown.

The coming of the Oxford, Worcester and Wolverhampton Railway in 1852-3, followed by the Midland Railway in 1864, gave a further boost to the horticultural industry. Railways enabled produce to be delivered quickly to all parts of Great Britain. Plums such as Pershore Eggs and Victorias and fruit including apples and strawberries were grown in huge quantities. They were sent by rail to Glasgow, Plymouth, Cardiff and London, arriving within a few hours of being harvested, and in times past the Evesham stations were frantically busy until late in the evening with growers bringing in their produce for loading.

Although the soil of the Vale of Evesham is good and the weather favourable, a great deal of the success of the agriculture in this area must be put down to the skill and dexterity of the small growers, many of whom made a living from only about five acres. This expertise in land management was spurred on by the arrangement for land tenancy known as the 'Evesham Custom'. The latter originated in 1872 when a number of the tenants of market garden land, owned by the squire, Charles Rudge, were given notice to vacate their grounds. These tenants having planted fruit trees and made many other improvements were now to be left without a livelihood. Banding together, they elected one of their company, Joseph Masters of Bengeworth, to negotiate with the squire. This he did with great skill and diplomacy. (Copies of his correspondence with Charles Rudge are in the Almonry Museum.) The outcome was the Evesham Custom which had the backing of an act of Parliament. The following paragraph concerning the Evesham Custom is taken from The LBG Story by Charles A. Binyon:

> As its name indicates The Evesham Custom is unique to the Vale of Evesham in its origin. The system of land tenure arose out of the vital needs of growers in and around Evesham. Under the Custom (restricted to market gardens) valuation of tenant-right takes into account the potential value of intense cultivation, unexhausted manures in the soil, all growing plants and trees and tenant's improvements. Thus, because he is almost as secure as a freeholder, the tenant can safely develop his holding. He also has the right to nominate a new tenant to the landlord at any time.

This had a great influence on the way the growers managed their land and holdings. Even the land under the fruit trees was utilised by growing daffodils, narcissi, gillies (wallflowers) and sweet williams for the markets. The womenfolk did much of this work and a good deal of the produce was sent away on commission, direct to the large towns.

Auctioneers were encouraged to hold markets and Joseph Masters was one of the prime instigators in obtaining the right for these markets to be held in the Market Place and in the High Street. This was of great benefit to growers and buyers. In 1881 Harvey Hunt had the foresight to erect sheds on land near the station at the far end of High Street for the purpose of selling the growers' produce by auction. It was known as the Smithfield Market and flourished until the 1970s when the decline of the market gardening industry made it necessary to change the ways of marketing. Mills & Green opened a market in 1983 and expanded when the Smithfield Market was gutted by fire in 1986 and closed down. However, gone are the days when horses and carts, and then lorries, laden with fruit and vegetables queued up outside the markets to unload their produce for sale to the highest bidder.

Another market was opened on land in Avon Street by F. G. & E.W. Beck in 1902. This was a very busy market and was a fascinating place for the young children living in that area who would listen to and watch the auctioneer at work, selling the vast mountains of produce piled up under the sheds. Alas this market declined and, being no longer viable, was closed down. The premises are now used as a market for selling a variety of bric-a-brac, vegetables, meat and so on, the stalls being rented out to individual people, the market providing an attraction for visitors to the town.

In the first decade of this century falling prices and high railway charges led Charles A. Binyon, a grower, to encourage other growers to form a co-operative, the Littleton & Badsey Growers' Association, which allowed them to buy requisites at a more competitive rate and to sell their produce at better prices. The growers were inspired to grow crops to a higher standard and to package their produce more attractively. They each bought shares in the company and in 1908 there were 35 members. This membership rose to 1,400 by

1958. Eventually the growers bought their own premises and transport, the produce being packaged and sent away daily.

At the beginning of the century so much fruit and vegetables were grown that canning and jam factories were needed to deal with them. Smedley's, Beaches' and Idiens' were kept very busy during the season, providing employment for many people living on the estates in and around Evesham. Beaches' diversified into the soft-drink industry but this firm has now ceased to trade. The import of exotic fruit and vegetables after the Second World War gradually saw the demise of the canning and jam industries. Smedley's has closed and the land has been used for a large Tesco store while Idiens' is no longer in business.

Fruit orchards were ripped up and glass cloches and then Dutch lights were used to obtain crops just a week or two earlier to get higher prices. Glasshouses multiplied, followed by plastic tunnels. Dutchmen, well-practised in the art of salad-crop growing under glass, came to the area, as did Italians. Chinese people have also come into the locality, growing for their restaurants and take-away food establishments. Mechanisation and high-tech growing are now the order of the day and very few of the old market gardening families are still working the land, much of it being put down to cereal crops or left fallow.

Now the fruit and vegetables grown in the Vale are an attraction for visitors who come to the area to purchase local produce from the numerous farm shops and 'pick your own' farms during the long harvest season. Other visitors come to the Vale to follow the blossom trail in spring while some find Evesham an excellent base for touring the surrounding district. The River Avon appeals to both the angling and the boating fraternity with narrow boats for hire and a pleasure trip boat operating from the town. History enthusiasts are enthralled by the remaining evidence of Evesham's rich past, such as the Bell Tower and the Almonry Museum, while the name of Simon de Montfort still draws travellers from far and wide. Whatever their reason for visiting this charming old town, those who stop awhile in Evesham find the experience very rewarding.

Churches and Chapels

1 This model of Evesham Abbey, made by Mr. T. Knight of Littleton, can be seen in the Almonry Museum. It gives a fairly accurate idea of what the abbey and its surroundings looked like in 1540, at the dissolution of Evesham Abbey. The ground plan of the abbey was reconstructed from information obtained during excavations carried out by Edward Rudge between 1811 and 1814.

2 Thought to date from the 14th century, the Evesham Abbey chair is made of oak and is 5 ft. 6in. high and 3 ft. 9 in. wide. Decorated with a band of vine branches interspersed with birds and quadrupeds carved around the back and arms, the back of the chair carries the arms of the abbey. The 16th-century quarter boys were once part of the clock mechanism installed in the Bell Tower. They turned on pivots to strike the bell on the hours.

3 A seal die of the late 11th century. The inscription has been effaced but the style of dress and of the workmanship suggests that this was the seal of one of the abbots of Evesham.

4 A page from a 14th-century psalter from Evesham Abbey showing the beautiful penmanship carried out in monastic times.

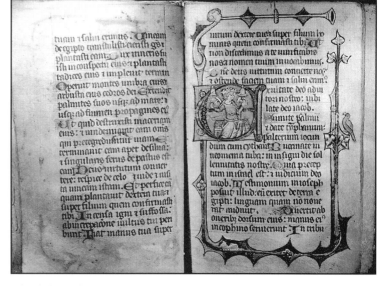

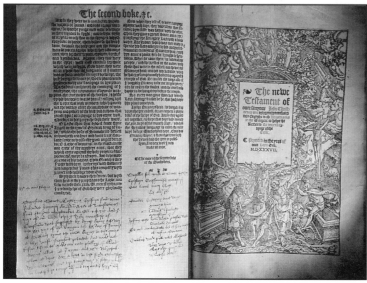

5 Bought by the Borough Council, the Matthew Bible of 1537 is housed in the Almonry Museum. It contains a hand-written account of the suppression of Evesham Abbey set down by one of the monks, John of Alcester.

6 Abbot Reginald's Gateway leads from the Market Place to the churchyard. Part of the gateway dates back to Norman times. It became customary during later times for the newly-elected abbot to be met by the monks at this spot. The abbot would remove his shoes and walk barefoot to the abbey church for his installation.

7 The almonry was part of the abbey, the first reference to an almoner at Evesham occurring *c.*1214. As the larger Benedictine monasteries were obliged to assist the poor, the almoner was allowed to distribute a tenth of all bread and beer which was made or bought within the abbey precinct. By the 14th century the almoner was required to seek out and relieve the sick and poor in their own homes. At the suppression of Evesham Abbey the almonry building was leased to the last abbot, Philip Hawford, for his life. It survived after his death as a private house, alterations being made to the building at intervals until the 18th century. The almonry was sold by the Rudge family to Evesham Corporation in 1929, which hoped one day to use the building as a museum. The Vale of Evesham Historical Society was formed in 1950 and the Almonry Museum opened in 1957, with the Society as honorary curators.

8 In 1664 the main part of the estate made up of the former abbey lands in Evesham came into the possession of Edward Rudge. He was the first 'Squire Rudge' of Evesham, representing the borough in Parliament. Another Edward Rudge (1763-1846) built Abbey Manor in 1817 and set about making extensive excavations of Evesham Abbey. His son, also named Edward Rudge (1792-1861), assisted in the excavating and compiled a history of Evesham, published in 1820. Fragments of the remains of Evesham Abbey were set up in the Abbey Manor grounds.

9 The Cloister Arch is one of the few remaining visible reminders of the fabric of the abbey. This illustration by Valentine Green can be seen in the Almonry Museum.

10 All Saints and St Lawrence, Evesham's two parish churches, share the same churchyard. Nearby is the abbey Bell Tower, a particularly fine building. Erected by Abbot Clement Lichfield and completed in 1538 just before the dissolution of the abbey, the tower had a dual purpose which was to house the abbey bells and to be the gatehouse to the abbey cemetery. At the dissolution the Bell Tower is reputed to have been sold to the townspeople for £100. In perpendicular style and 110ft. high, it is generally considered to be the last complete pre-Reformation ecclesiastical building in the country. The Bell Tower now has a ring of 14 bells which is thought to be one of the best in the land.

11 The Lichfield Chapel is to be found in the church of St Lawrence and is thought to have been built by Clement Lichfield between 1500 and 1509. Graceful fan tracery of perpendicular style with Tudor emblems make this chantry very beautiful.

12 This view, taken in Vine Street, shows the Church Parade passing the Town Hall on its way to the site of the abbey on 9 May 1909. The procession was part of the commemoration festival held to celebrate the 1,200th anniversary of the foundation of the abbey. A number of other events took place at this time, the Church House was dedicated and opened, a branch of the Mothers' Union was formed and a choir festival was held, with 12 local choirs processing from the Bell Tower to All Saints Church. A hymn, 'God our Strength' was especially written and composed for the occasion. Commemorative medals, showing the Bell Tower on one side and the arms of the abbey on the other, were distributed to those who took part in the festival.

13 As most of the early Quakers were prominent members of the business community, they met secretly for many years before building the Friends' Meeting House, being the first nonconformists to build a purpose-built meeting place in the town. A burial ground used exclusively by the Quakers is situated at the rear of the building and is still in use today.

14 Built for the Presbyterians in 1759, the Oat Street Chapel, apart from enlargement in 1862, has remained virtually unchanged in appearance. During the 19th century the building was taken over by the Unitarians, as their movement gained momentum in the town. Many prominent people of Evesham worshipped there including the New family and George May.

15 From its early beginnings Methodism has always had a strong following in Evesham, with the Wesleys preaching in the town on numerous occasions. The first Methodist church was built in Capon Pot Lane (later known as Chapel Street), opening in 1808. As numbers grew a larger building was needed, the foundation stone of which was laid at a stone-laying ceremony held in 1906. The church adjacent to the Workman Bridge was completed and opened in 1907.

16 The Mayor and the Town Corporation proceed down Bridge Street to the opening of the new Methodist Church.

17 St Mary's Roman Catholic Church, a corrugated iron building, was situated next to the substantial, stone-built Catholic school. It was here that the marriage of Princess Louise d'Orleans to Prince Charles de Bourbon-Siciles was solemnised in 1907. When the new church was built the old building was moved to Pershore, where it was used as a builder's shed.

18 A crowd gathered for the laying of the foundation stone of the new Roman Catholic church in Evesham.

Souvenir of the
Opening of the New Church

19   St Mary's, the new Roman Catholic church, was opened in 1907.

20 St Peter's Church, Bengeworth. This church was probably built by the abbots of Evesham Abbey at the end of the 12th century. By 1870 it had fallen into such a state of disrepair that it was decided to demolish it and replace it with a new church. It was then found that the walls were so strong that explosives had to be used to demolish them!

21 The new St Peter's Church was built, in 1872, at what is now the junction of Elm Road, Kings Road and Broadway Road. The building is of local blue Lias limestone dressed with Bath stone. The spire is 133 ft. high.

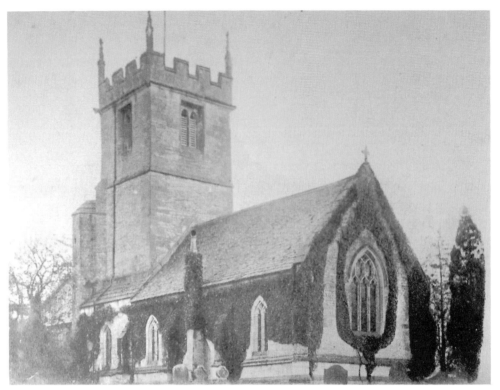

22 St Andrew's Church, Hampton is unique among the churches in the Vale of Evesham as it has a large central tower which suggests an earlier Norman church. The chancel was rebuilt in 1282 and further work took place in the 15th century, when the building was enlarged to its present form.

23 Salvation Army Band, *c.*1910. The cornet player seated in the front row is Mr. C. Martin. The band was often heard playing on what is now the parking area outside Carpenter's in the High Street.

The Town

24 Workman Bridge replaced the earlier narrow, medieval, eight-arched structure which linked Bengeworth with Evesham. The original plans were for a metal suspension bridge. £9,200 was raised towards building the bridge, but estimates of the final cost rocketed. New plans were drawn up and the present, three-arched, stone bridge was built at an estimated cost of £13,000. The bridge carries a plaque to commemorate Henry Workman's part in its construction.

25 A crowded Bridge Street viewed from the centre of Workman Bridge.

26 Charles (Fozzie) Pickering, a well-known local porter, pushes his truck up Bridge Street. Tommy Evans' shop was on the opposite corner to the Worcester Co-operative shop which is now a restaurant. Hodgetts' toy shop is no more and the premises are now part of the modern Bridge Court complex.

27 George Mason's grocer's shop was located next door to the Midland Bank in Bridge Street. It was very busy and had a staff of twenty-five or more. Left to right in the back row of this 1937 photograph are J. Eales and H. Hughes. Standing in the middle row are J. Sewell (inspector), E. Wilkes (van driver), R. Beagley, F. Hitchcock, A. Raines, J. Stevens, J. Maycock, H. Grove, K. Newman, S. Underhill, J. Vernall, E. Bailey (van driver), Campbell's representative and R. Reeves. The front row comprises C. Tucker, W. Wootton, F. Checketts, J. Robbins, R. Wagstaffe (manager), Miss Cath Lane, B. J. Rouse and N. Forrest.

28 Lowe and Sons were to be found in Orleans House in Bridge Street *c.*1900. They were linen drapers and silk mercers who specialised in ready-to-wear and made-to-order ladies' fashions.

29 Among the shops at the High Street end of Bridge Street were the tea and refreshment rooms of F. C. Byrd, where at the beginning of this century one could obtain one of his celebrated Evesham Hunt Pork Pies. Langstone House, the building between Byrd's and Mayer's, has a greater claim to fame though, for in 1644 Charles I stayed and held court there during the Civil War.

30 The Round House features prominently in this view of Bridge Street taken from its junction with High Street, as does the Evesham Journal building belonging to W. & H. Smith.

31 The Round House was probably built as a dwelling house *c*.1450, but by the 16th century it was listed as an inn. It was subsequently converted into shops and solicitors' offices, as can be seen in this view of the Bridge Street end of the building. It was bought by the National Provincial Bank in 1919, although the shops and offices were retained. The Round House was extensively restored in 1963 and is now owned by the National Westminster Bank.

32 The Market Place, *c*.1875. Vegetables, cereals, wool, cloth, clothing, leather goods, boots and shoes were offered for sale in the Market Place. In the latter half of the 19th century market tolls were collected in an office to the left of the Round House. The alley to the right of the Round House, leading to Bridge Street, was renamed Melsungen Allee when Evesham was twinned with the German town of Melsungen.

33 This view shows the Market Place decorated for the coronation of Edward VII in 1902. The Round House is on the left while the building that was to become the Public Hall is on the right.

34 A luncheon was held to celebrate the opening of the new Public Hall on Wednesday, 14 April 1909. Guests included the Mayors of Evesham, Worcester and Stratford, Colonel Long M.P., the directors of the builders Espley & Co., the Vicar of Evesham and councillors. They tucked into a meal that included salmon mayonnaise, lamb, sirloin of beef, chicken, York ham, boeuf à la mode, lemon soufflé, plum tart, stewed rhubarb with custard and cheese and biscuits.

Borough of Evesham.

LUNCHEON

ON THE OCCASION OF
THE

Opening of the Public Hall

ON

WEDNESDAY APRIL 14TH, 1909.

C. F. COX,
Mayor.

THOS. A. COX,
Town Clerk.

35 This view of the Town Hall taken from Vine Street *c*.1841 shows the rear of the hall with open arches, the old town jail, which has long been demolished, and Tommy Wheeler's builder's yard, which was on the site of the present-day Allen's newsagents.

36 This corner of the Market Place *c*.1890 was home to a number of businesses. H. Goodall started his business as a farrier and general smith, graduating to carriage-making. His premises were demolished in 1908 to extend the Public Hall. Goodall moved to the High Street, expanding his expertise to cater for the new horseless carriages. The business is still going strong, selling motor cars from near the railway station. Next door to Goodall's was the *Red Lion Inn*, one of a number of inns in Evesham from which local carriers ran their services, taking people and goods to and from the local villages. The premises of W. Cook, who was agent for the South Wales & Cannock Chase Coal & Coke Co. Ltd., were next to the *Red Lion*. Across the alley was the Walker Hall, housing the hairdressing business of J. G. Billings. Adjacent to the Walker Hall was the Post Office, which was situated in the Market Place from 1883 to 1960.

37 This is the rear of the *Red Lion Inn* in the Market Place. It was demolished to make way for the extension of the Public Hall.

38 Restored in 1916, this alley was once known as The Shambles, but is now named Allée de Dreux after the town in France with which Evesham is twinned. The *Volunteer* public house on the right of the picture is no more and today a shoe shop occupies the premises.

39 These tea-rooms in The Shambles were owned by Ralph Harris.

40 Manchester House, the premises of R. W. Righton, milliner and costumier, which stood on the corner of Bewdley Street and High Street, was demolished in 1931 to widen the road to cater for increased traffic. A new building, with the same name, was erected with a curved frontage. Today the premises are used for a carpet shop.

41 The Mayor and Corporation, wearing their Jubilee medals, parade in the High Street following the election of Mr. Isaac Morris as the new mayor in 1887. The clock on the Town Hall, seen in the background, was built to celebrate Queen Victoria's Golden Jubilee. It was affectionately known as 'Old Emma', after the wife of Isaac Morris. A fountain and barometer were later added to the building to commemorate the Queen's Diamond Jubilee in 1897.

42 The gentlemen in the doorway of this butcher's shop belonging to the Byrd family are Mr. Abel, on the left, and Mr. Bearcroft. Still in use as a butcher's shop and now run by Collins and Grindle, the shop front has remained practically unchanged for most of this century.

43 Dresden House was built *c*.1692 by Robert Cookes, who was an attorney and steward of the Rudge Estate and also a Mayor of Evesham. His second daughter, Elizabeth, married Dr. William Baylies, who despite inheriting a considerable fortune on her early death, had problems with creditors. Taking up residence on the continent, he became physician to the ageing Frederick the Great of Prussia. Dresden House was sold to meet his debts. In the course of time, the property was occupied by the Evesham Bank of Messrs. Oldaker, Day, Lavender and Murrell of which Mr. Lavender was manager. Known as the Old Bank, it failed in 1829. After Mr. Lavender's death, business was carried on at Dresden House by Mr. Beasley. an ironmonger. When he vacated the premises, Mrs. Lavender moved back and took in paying guests. Her daughter, Mrs. Frances Farrell, opened a school there for young ladies in 1860 and this school continued to flourish into the next century. Dresden House then became a gentlemen's club, but this closed a while ago and there is now a restaurant on the premises.

44 George Grove stands by the unusual sundial installed by Robert Cookes in the garden of Dresden House. At least three gnomons, which show the hour of the day by their shadows, are visible on the pillar. The sundial is topped by an iron weathercock with a metal pennant which is perforated with Robert Cookes' initials and the date 1720.

45 Laden charabancs are waiting in the High Street outside the International Stores, now the premises of Midlands Electricity.

46 The High Street in Evesham is very wide. It was used in the 19th century for a weekly cattle market. This continued until 1880 when a purpose-built cattle market was constructed. The three-storeyed house next to Eccles' was later turned into the Scala and then the Clifton cinema. It is now a bingo hall.

47 On the wall above the door of A. W. Wheatley's shop was a plaque showing the establishment's appointment as shoemaker to the Duc d'Orleans family of Wood Norton. The shop, which was on the west side of High Street, was demolished around 1903.

48 These old cottages next to Almswood in the High Street were demolished to make way for offices and part of the new Post Office, which was built in 1960.

49 Almswood, an 18th-century mansion, is believed to be the oldest surviving house in the High Street. The building has housed the Unitarian ministers, the Rev. Timothy Davis and later on his brother the Rev. David Davis, Miss Clark's School in 1914, a branch of the United Counties Bank, an Inland Revenue Office, the home, surgery and dispensary of W. Manley Savery and his brother, and at present the offices of an accountant.

50 An artist's impression and the architect's plans drawn in 1890 showed how the new terrace in the High Street would look. Situated between the Roman Catholic church and Leicester Grove, the houses are now nearly all used as offices. The Town Council offices are situated here.

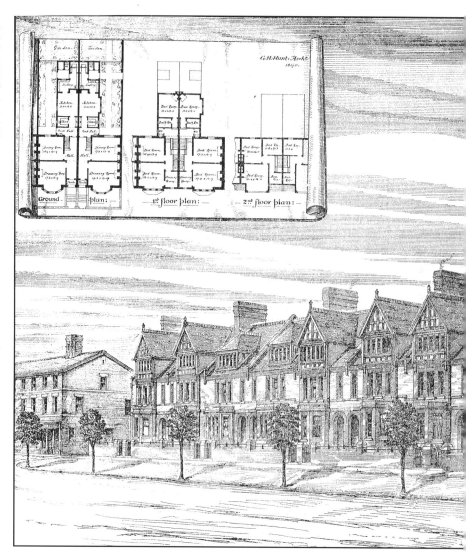

51 This photograph shows a busy scene at the top end of the High Street, looking towards Greenhill. On the right can be seen the wall fronting the Smithfield Market, with the *Railway Hotel* beyond it. On the left is the entrance to the Midland Railway's goods yard and beyond that, opposite the *Railway Hotel*, is the entrance to the G.W.R. and M.R. stations. The *Railway Hotel* was built between the Great Western and Midland Railway lines which pass under the High Street at this spot.

STREET TERRACE :
EVESHAM :

52 Children posed for the camera in this 1897 photograph of houses in Cambria Road, which is situated off Greenhill. The gentleman in the wheelchair was Mr. Thacker.

53 J. M. Stokes, whose warehouse and offices were in Swan Lane, was one of the largest fruit and vegetable merchants in Evesham. The firm gave a large number of people employment on its farms and loading and driving its lorries. Today the site is occupied by the Gateway supermarket.

54 These houses stood at the Four Corners, the junction of Cowl Street, Oat Street, Chapel Street and Mill Street, c.1903. Those nearest the camera are good examples of timber-framed town houses with overhanging upper storeys. As well as giving more room upstairs, these overhangs or jetties were structural features. The weight of the upper walls and the roof on the ends of the overhanging joists counterbalanced the weight of all the furniture in the upstairs rooms which tended to make joists sag in the middle. The two houses on the nearest corner can still be seen, the rest have gone.

55 Harding's fish shop was situated underneath the front of the Town Hall. The assistants were always attired in blue and white striped aprons and straw boaters.

56 The residents of Bewdley Street are enjoying their 1911 Coronation Dinner.

57 Vine Street was formerly known as Swine Street as it was used as a venue for selling pigs. The Almonry can be seen in the distance.

58 This building in Vine Street was once a merchant's house. White's, a wheelwright's shop, was situated in the right-hand corner, which is now the entrance to Vine Mews.

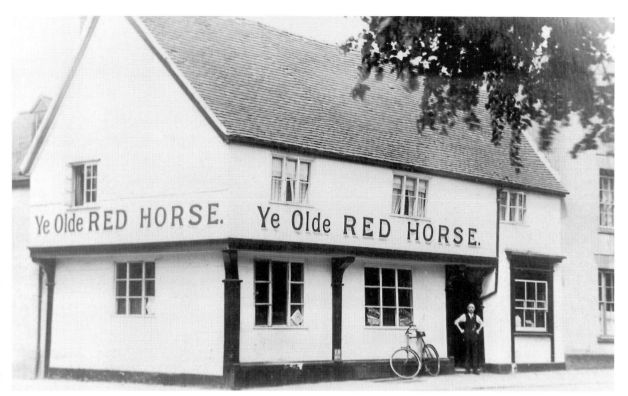

59 *Ye Olde Red Horse* is to be found in Vine Street, opposite the Almonry. It was covered in stucco until 1932, when the walls were stripped to reveal the 16th-century timbers.

60 The age of the building and its proximity to the Abbey Gatehouse suggests that the *Trumpet Inn* on Merstow Green possibly dates back to monastic times. T. J. S. Baylis, who has researched the licensed trade in Evesham, surmises that the name of the inn could be derived from the trumpet that the Angel Gabriel carried and that the sign was used to attract pilgrims to the inn.

61 Ladies in their best hats sit at a table piled-high with party fare at the Merstow Green Coronation Dinner of 1911.

62 Mr. and Mrs. Taylor are pictured outside the cottages at the side of All Saints' and St Lawrence's churchyard. The cottages were situated between Vine Street and the Walker Hall, fronting on to Strangers' Piece, where people not of the town were buried. The site of the cottages later became the location of Coulter's car showroom and is now part of the Abbey Gates Shopping Centre.

63 These cottages were situated at the bottom of Conduit Hill, near the gas works and the meat-processing factory of Collins Brothers.

64 Evesham has always been well-endowed with licensed premises. In 1841 there were forty-two! The *Angel Inn* at the corner of Port Street and Castle Street has survived from 1841 although it has since changed names a number of times. It has been known as the *Old Angel*, *The Angel Inn* and is now called the *Angel Vaults*. It was one of the public houses owned by the Evesham brewers, Sladden and Collier.

65 Mrs. Wheatley stands in the doorway of Handel Wheatley's ironmongery and fancy goods shop in Port Street. This establishment has recently ceased trading after more than a century.

66 The 'Port Street Observatory', *c.*1905. This unusual building in Port Street was built by one of the Burlingham family to house an astronomical telescope.

67 Mrs. Ethel Mary Knott stands outside her husband, Dennis Knott's workshop in The Leys. He was a sanitary plumber and house decorator and later established the caravan site on the banks of the river, now known as Weir Meadow Holiday Park.

68 Nail-makers plied their trade in Citroen Terrace, commonly known as Nailers' Row. The workshops were rented or owned by nail merchants such as Burlingham and Co., Mr. Jos. Gilbert and Mr. Twyning. They charged the nail-makers one shilling per week for coal and one penny per week for the use of forge and tools. The nail-makers were supplied with ½cwt. of iron from which they were expected to produce 45lb. of horse-nails. Finished nails were loaded into baskets and shipped from the river wharves.

69 A horse refreshes itself at the water trough erected at the junction of Port Street, Broadway Road, Elm Road and Kings Road. The row of houses behind the driver of the trap are in Elm Road. These houses and those visible in Kings Road to the left were built at the turn of the century.

70 These old houses were on Waterside next door to the *Northwick Arms. The Park View Hotel* now stands in their place.

71   Walking along Waterside, in the snow, towards Coopers Lane.

72   The Workman Pleasure Grounds were constructed between Waterside and the river when the new Workman Bridge was built. Dredgings from below the bridge were used to build up the level of the land. This wintry scene shows the band stand and the Jawbones Arch which was presented to the borough in 1906 by Mrs. Frances Edwards, the grand-daughter of Dr. Thomas Beale Cooper.

73 The Jawbones Arch originally stood in the grounds of the Mansion House, at the corner of Coopers Lane and Waterside. The whale's jawbones were presented to Dr. Beale Cooper by his friend Mr. Stanton, who had assisted in the capture of the whale whilst aboard the ship *Andrew Marvel* in 1820. They were dispatched to Evesham from Hull and Dr. Beale Cooper is reported to have been presented with the bill for their carriage!

74 Present-day Coopers Lane leads from Church Street and Owletts End to Waterside. It runs by the side of the Mansion House and was originally known as Watson Lane. It was later known as Beale Cooper Lane.

75 The Mansion House in Bengeworth was built by Thomas Watson soon after he bought the land at the dissolution of Evesham Abbey in 1540. The house was subsequently enlarged by Thomas Beale Cooper between 1810 and 1812. It became a hotel in 1926 and is currently known as the *Evesham Hotel*.

76 The *Hampton House Hotel* was run by Miss Frances Greenwood who had previously been at the *Hotel Bonear* in Port Street. The *Hampton House Hotel* offered its guests croquet lawns, tennis, boating and garage facilities. During the Second World War the hotel was requisitioned for use by B.B.C. staff who had been evacuated to Wood Norton. After the war the B.B.C. retained it as an engineering training centre. The house is now part of an industrial estate.

77 The large house on the right belonged to Frank Enstone. The site is now the car park of the Working Men's Club at Hampton. Workman Road was made between Mr. Enstone's house and the row of houses which are set back from Pershore Road.

The River

78 The steamer *Lily* was well-known in Evesham at the beginning of this century. She belonged to Charles Byrd of the *Fleece Inn* which once stood at the bottom of Bridge Street. Later the *Lily* was altered and, as the *Lilybyrd*, she remained a familiar sight on the Avon for many years.

79 The *Diamond Queen* was another steam launch operated on the river by Charles Byrd. Trips ran from near the *Fleece Inn* originally, but in later years ran from the Tower View Café and River Gardens which were further downstream on the opposite bank. Here there was a 500ft. river frontage and 500 people could be seated in comfort for luncheons and teas. In later years, besides the *Diamond Queen* and the *Lilybyrd*, the motor launches *Diana*, registered to carry 26 passengers, and *Nancy Jo*, for parties up to 12, could be hired.

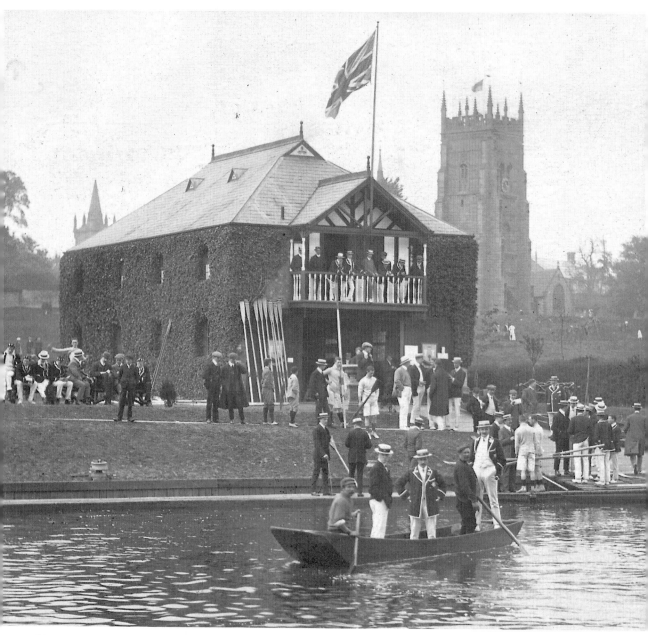

80 Evesham Rowing Club boathouse. The Evesham Boat Club was founded in June 1863 for the purpose of holding a Regatta at Evesham to coincide with the Agricultural and Horticultural Shows on 23 September 1863. The Boat Club's first headquarters was a wooden shed with a 'hard' in front for launching the boats. This was situated 75 yds. below Evesham Bridge, opposite the Workman Pleasure Grounds. The club moved into their present boathouse about 1890.

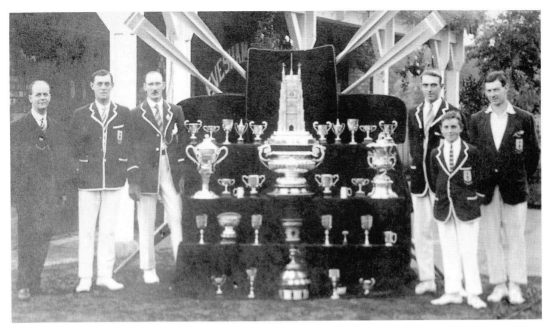

81 Rowing Club trophies. The 1863 Regatta was a great success and soon became an annual event. The Boat Club became known as the Rowing Club and Evesham as the 'Henley of the Midlands'. The principal prize was the Vale of Evesham Challenge Trophy, a silver model of the Bell Tower. This trophy was stolen in 1966 and has never been recovered.

82 On their annual outing of 15 August 1911, the Evesham Master Bakers travelled from Evesham to Worcester aboard the steam launch, *Swallow*, which was owned by the boatbuilder, Bathurst of Tewkesbury. She was part of a pleasure boat fleet which included the steamers *River King*, *River Queen* and *Jubilee*. The Master Bakers were photographed at Upper Strensham Mill on the Lower Avon. In the background can be seen the mill house and Strensham Lock.

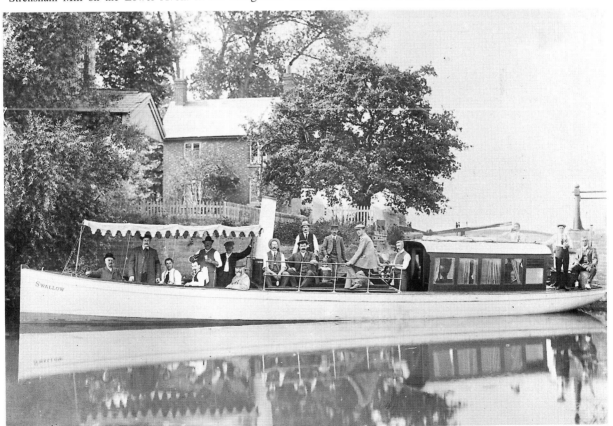

83 On 1 July 1910 the workforce of Willmotts' enjoyed their annual outing aboard the *River Queen* of Tewkesbury. The company based on Conduit Hill have employed local people for many years and are still in business producing spectacle cases and presentation boxes for jewellery.

84 The ferry crossing between Evesham and Hampton was used for centuries by the monks at Evesham Abbey, as their vineyard was on the terraced slope above the ferry. In the early years of the century it cost a ha'penny for a return fare on the rope ferry. The price increased to one penny in the 1930s while in the 1990s it costs 30p each way. From Evesham the way to the ferry is along Boat Lane.

85 Glover's Island is named after Frank Glover. A cooper by trade, he was a quarrelsome man who would pick fights in the town and then adjourn to the island, near the now-demolished Midland Railway bridge, for the contest. The island was apparently in 'no man's land' between the Worcestershire and Gloucestershire constabularies, so the fights were able to proceed without interference from the police.

86 Access to Glover's Island was hazardous. Here we see an Edwardian lady crossing to the island on what appears to be a fallen tree trunk. The pollarded willows are still a common site along the banks of the Avon.

87 The River Avon is prone to flood after heavy rain, as the inhabitants of Waterside and the lower end of Port Street have found to their cost. On Sunday, 30 December 1900, 3.14 in. of rain were recorded within 24 hours. By the Monday morning the meadows, the Workman Pleasure Grounds and the low-lying parts of Bengeworth had been inundated. The river rose 15 ft. by the afternoon of the last day of the year.

88 The Workman Bridge was an excellent viewpoint for observing the 'New Century Flood'. The people of Evesham were able to take advantage of this, but not those in Bengeworth, as the water was too deep at the junction of Waterside and Port Street to allow pedestrian traffic through.

89 Water poured out of Castle Street 'like a river', with a current so strong that some horses refused to pass through the flood.

90 Waterside was badly hit by the New Century Flood. In some places the water reached a depth of six ft. New houses erected in place of the old cottages near the *Northwick Arms* were supposed to have been built above any possible flood level, as no flood since 1856 had reached that high. In that year the new bridge had been built and the aits and osier beds below the bridge had been dredged away. It was thought that these had restricted the flow of the river and caused the high floods in the past but unfortunately the new flood-proof houses were inundated to a depth of 1ft. 6in.

91 The New Century Flood was the highest on record since 1848, but the river regularly reached, and still reaches, Waterside as this view looking along Waterside shows. Not quite so deep on this occasion in 1908, waggons were still able to negotiate the flood waters. In 1993 the river reached across the road which had to be closed, as modern motor cars were unable to cope!

92 A later flood scene at Waterside. The old fountain has been moved to the other end of Port Street, near the church, and has been replaced by a more mundane sign post.

Sports and Recreation

93 The *Vauxhall Inn* in Abbey Road had its own successful Angling Society. The Avon at Evesham was and still is the venue for important angling competitions.

94 The Avon freezes over in hard winters. This group of skaters, pictured near Hampton Ferry, had taken advantage of the frozen river, having probably skated downriver from the Abbey Park.

95 The Mayor of Evesham, Mr. J. Felton, called a meeting in the Town Hall in 1911 for the purpose of forming a Swimming and Water Polo Club. Mr. E. Tarry was elected Captain of the Club which used the river for many years until the old, open air baths were built at Common Road. These have now been replaced by an indoor pool in Davies Road.

96 Mr. Hirons is second from the left in this group playing bowls. There was a bowling green on the Abbey Park from the turn of the century but it ceased to exist when the Abbey Gates Shopping Centre was built. The Bowling Club had been in decline for a number of years but it is now undergoing a considerable revival. A new site has recently been acquired next to the cricket pavilion and a bowling green was opened there in 1993.

97 The Evesham Boys' Club soccer team, 1931-2. This team played in the North Cotswold League and competed in the Hospital Cup.

98 Evesham Hockey Club 1909-10. Left to Right: Ladyman, Palethorpe, V. C. Cliffe, Bob Rowland, V. C. Hill, Mark Warner, Harrison, A. W. Rowbotham, Gordon Hill, R. H. Burlingham, Raymond Hodgkinson, Charles Fowler, Alfred Cliffe, A. G. Phillips (secretary).

99 Louis Newbury, father of local singer and broadcaster Vic Newbury, was a member of this local cricket team which played against a side led by the famous cricketer, W. G. Grace.

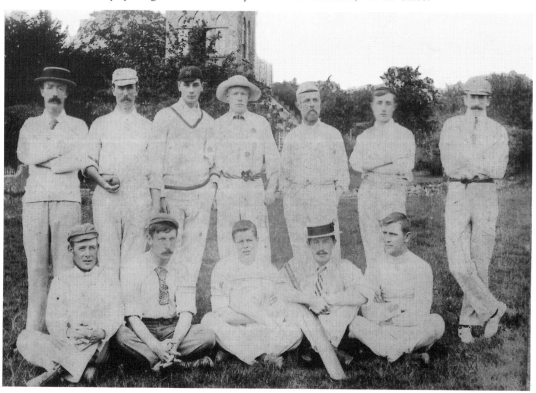

100 The well-patronised Evesham Amateur Dramatic Society performed 'Uncles and Aunts' (as produced at the Comedy Theatre, London!), on Easter Wednesday 1891. The cast list included members of some of Evesham's well-known families.

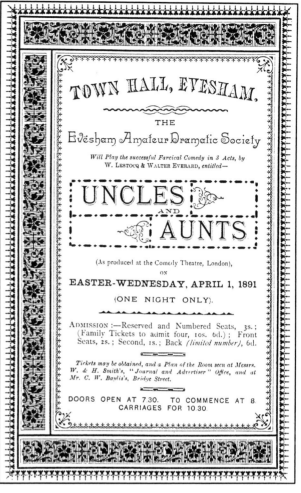

TOWN HALL, EVESHAM.

THE

Evesham Amateur Dramatic Society

Will Play the successful Farcical Comedy in 3 Acts, by
W. LESTOCQ & WALTER EVERARD, entitled—

UNCLES
AND
AUNTS

(As produced at the Comedy Theatre, London),
ON
EASTER-WEDNESDAY, APRIL 1, 1891

(ONE NIGHT ONLY).

ADMISSION :—Reserved and Numbered Seats, 3s.;
(Family Tickets to admit four, 10s. 6d.) ; Front
Seats, 2s. ; Second, 1s. ; Back (limited number), 6d.

Tickets may be obtained, and a Plan of the Room seen at Messrs.
W. & H. Smith's, "Journal and Advertiser" Office, and at
Mr. C. W. Baylis's, Bridge Street.

DOORS OPEN AT 7.30. TO COMMENCE AT 8.
CARRIAGES FOR 10.30.

101 The charter of 1605 authorised the holding of three fairs a year in Evesham, including two statute fairs held on the Friday before and after old Michaelmas Day. These statute fairs were known as Mop Fairs and it was at these fairs that farm and domestic workers were hired. The second fair or the 'Runaway Mop' was held for the benefit of those workers who were not satisfied with arrangements made at the first Mop. Over the years the nature of these fairs changed and, as can be seen, by the turn of the century the fairs had a large 'fun-fair' element. The 'Hurry-Skurry' appears to have been a popular attraction.

102 The 'toy railway' at this Mop Fair jumped the gun by almost a century, proclaiming itself to be the 'Great Channel Tunnel Railway'. Mop Fairs are still held on Merstow Green, despite opposition from some of the local residents, but are now purely fun-fairs.

103 In 1909 an Old English Fête was held in the Workman Pleasure Grounds. As we can see from this picture of the hoop-la stall, the stallholders dressed up in 'old English' costumes!

Hospitals

104 Evesham Cottage Hospital was substantially supported by the Evesham Hospital Galas which were started in 1928. A report in the *Evesham Journal* of November 1929 stated that the Gala Committee had raised £2,851 4s. 1d. in the two years they had been functioning. Mr. C. N. Mason, a local bank manager, was King Carnival but a different Queen was chosen every year. This picture shows the King holding the hand of the matron, Miss E. M. Terrill, outside Evesham Cottage Hospital.

105 The Evesham Hospital Galas were very colourful and received tremendous support from Evesham people and the surrounding villages. Special trains were run to bring people to the spectacle. During the week King Carnival and his court visited places in the locality and held various functions to swell the funds. Many of the local dignitaries and prominent families gave their support and an ox was roasted, slices being sold by auction.

EVESHAM HOSPITAL GALA WEEK.

Programme of

COMMUNITY SINGING
CONCERT

SUNDAY, SEPTEMBER 9th, 1928,

IN THE

ABBEY PARK.

MASSED BANDS & CHOIRS

Conductor:

Mr. A. M. SLATTER, A.R.C.O.

GIVE LIBERALLY to the OFFICIAL COLLECTORS.

PRICE   ONE PENNY.

106 On Sunday, 9 September 1928, during the Hospital Gala Week, the townsfolk of Evesham were entertained in the Abbey Park by massed bands and choirs led by their conductor, Mr. A. M. Slatter. The musical programme included favourites such as God Save The King, Lead Kindly Light, Land of Hope and Glory, Drink To Me Only and Abide With Me.

107 The Cottage Hospital was built in Briar Close in the 1920s.

108 This photograph commemorates the visit to Evesham Cottage Hospital made by Queen Amelie of Portugal during her stay with her brother, the Duc d'Orleans, who lived at Wood Norton.

109 At the top of Kings Road was the Sanatorium, where people with the often-fatal diseases of diphtheria and scarlet fever were isolated. This view shows the West Ward. Mrs. Martin, who worked there, recalled collecting patients in a horse and cart. Visitors were not allowed into the Sanatorium but had to talk to the patients through a window. When the hospital closed, the building became a laboratory for the Agricultural Development and Advisory Service.

110 Abbey Manor, the home of the Rudge family, was used as a military hospital during the First World War. The Red Cross Commandant of the 25-bed hospital was Mrs. F. Haynes Rudge.

111 Nursing staff and patients pose for a photograph outside the Red Cross Military Hopital at Abbey Manor.

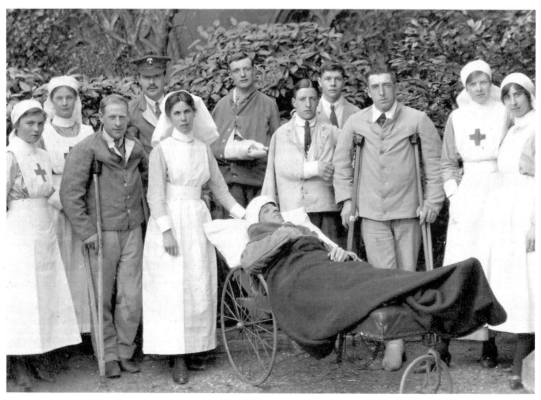

Growing

112 In times past Evesham was a spectacular sight at blossom time as, right up until after the Second World War, plum-growing was a major part of the market gardening industry.

113 The Spiers' Evesham Wonder is a variety of plum developed by the Spiers, a well-known fruit-growing family.

114 Very long ladders were needed to pick the plums and men strapped their willow baskets on to strong leather belts, leaving both hands free for picking. Wages were about £1 10s. a week and much of the picking was piece-work. Many of the old plum trees have now disappeared. Newer varieties have been introduced to grow on smaller trees, making picking much easier.

115 Mr. Mills is pictured here selling Victoria plums at the Smithfield Market. Plums were sold in chip baskets made by the Besto Chip Factory in Elm Road, Bengeworth.

116 Mrs. C. Hirons and her daughter are weighing up the chips full of strawberries that they have gathered. Picking strawberries was a back-aching job, but the piece-work was a chance for the ladies to make a few extra shillings.

117 The women in this photograph are picking currants. In front of them is a row of bell cloches, which protected crops such as rhubarb from late frosts and enabled the growers to harvest the fruit just that little bit earlier, so making higher prices at market. Behind the women can be seen a row of plum trees.

118 Most cultivation of the ground was carried out by hand as labour was cheap. The men would dig the land beneath the fruit trees and were paid by the chain. They used an assortment of implements such as spades and two-, three- or four-tined forks.

119 Mr. Charles Martin Senior and a group which includes his four sons and two daughters are busy tying asparagus for market. Twenty buds were put into a round and six rounds put together to make a hundred (120 buds). This was then tied round with willow twigs to keep it firmly together. The 'gras', as it is locally known, was often cut twice a day if the weather was very hot.

Herefordshire and Worcestershire Agricultural Society.

EVESHAM MEETING, 1901.

Complimentary Dinner

TO THE

Officials, Judges and Stewards,

AT THE

FARMERS' HALL, EVESHAM,

On Monday Evening, June 10th, 1901.

CHAIRMAN - MR. GEOFFREY NEW.

(Chairman of the Local Committee.)

120 The Officials, Judges and Stewards of the Herefordshire and Worcestershire Agricultural Society were feasted at the Farmers' Hall, Evesham, in June 1901. They were entertained during the dinner by the 'Schartau Quartette Party'.

121 Mr. W. G. Carter of Bretforton won first prize in the 1907 Asparagus Show held in the Farmers' Hall, Evesham.

122 A wicker hamper full of 'champion', prize-winning asparagus grown by W. J. Newman of Hinton Cross, near Evesham. This illustration shows the way in which the asparagus was tied into rounds and then packed into the hampers for dispatch to all parts of the country.

123 For many years Evesham was the main area for the growing of early radishes. Seed would be sown in late December and early January and covered with straw to protect the young plants from frost. The womenfolk would help with the pulling of the radishes, which were then bunched, washed and put into hampers to be sold in the local markets. From there they were sent all over the country by train, often arriving in Manchester, London or Scotland the same day or early the next morning. Onions were drilled using either a Davis' or Gilbert's seed drill. When fully grown they were dug up by the men and taken to the hovels (sheds) for the women to tie and tag on a piece-work basis.

124 Many acres of peas were drilled in the area. Women and children, pea-picking to supplement their income, made a colourful sight. Often the children were kept from school to help swell the coffers. Fingers really flew, as they plucked the peas from the haulm, because the work was paid by results.

125 Pea-picking, between the river and Burford Road in Bengeworth, on land owned by James Bacon.

126 Lettuces cut for market were also packed into wicker hampers. Plastic bags and trays came much later!

127 Hampers of produce laid out ready for sale at the Central Market in Evesham which was run by Frank Beck.

128 E. G. Righton, Auctioneer and Estate Agent, standing by the railings with his papers and pipe, was a familiar face to all the wholesale agents who came from Birmingham, Wales and The North to buy Evesham produce.

129 Mr. Agg of Childs-wickham was one of the last Vale growers to take his produce to market with a horse and dray. He is seen here at the Smithfield Market in Evesham.

130 This aerial view shows Smedley's canning factory sandwiched between the Worcester Road and the extensive G.W.R. goods yard which is full of box vans used to convey produce from the Vale to distant destinations. The canning factory was owned by the Wisbech Produce Canners Ltd. in 1931.

131 In the past fruit and vegetable canning was a thriving but labour-intensive industry in the area. The advent of frozen produce reduced the need for so much labour and killed off the canning industry.

132   Littleton & Badsey Growers canned the produce of their members and sold the fruit and vegetables under their own label. This is their exhibit at the Imperial Fruit Show, *c*.1927.

133   Burlingham's wharf and yard, 1934. The Evesham firm of Burlingham & Co. traded in Evesham for almost 200 years from this site on the river. From this wharf Burlingham's shipped many of the nails made for them in Bengeworth down-river to Gloucester. The firm ceased trading in recent years, the site being taken over by Jewsons. The buildings, at the time of writing, are being demolished to make way for a development of riverside apartments.

134 The decline of nail-making and the growth of market gardening in the Vale led the family firm of Burlingham & Co. to develop the agricultural side of their business. This photograph of 1904 shows, standing from left to right, George Heally, Fred Webb, Will Heritage Snr., George Davies, possibly Jim Freeman, Will Heritage Jnr. and George Heritage. The name of the lad sitting on the binder is not known.

135 As well as selling machinery and tools to the local growers, Burlingham's also supplied fertilisers which they mixed on their premises, as this later view of 1952 shows.

Transport

136 John Andrews and son Jack are setting off for market with produce in pot hampers, *c.*1890.

137 The Martin family of Bengeworth are pictured in Lime Street preparing to take their produce to market with their horse and dray.

138 A Midland Red charabanc pauses on Waterside with a full complement of passengers, which includes Messrs. W. Byrd, S. Malin, H. Evans, A. Andrews, W. Winett, W. Herbert and G. Collins.

139 This appears to be a group of anglers preparing to depart from the *Old Angel Inn* in Brick-kiln Street. They seem to be well-provisioned with what is presumably a hamper of food tied to the roof of the lorry cab and a barrel of XXX strength beer in the passenger seat!

140 Coulter's Garage was originally in premises in the Market Place. The advent of the model T Ford made expansion a priority. This was achieved gradually, the firm eventually occupying nearly all of their side of the Market Place. Coulter's occupied the site until the building of the Abbey Gates Shopping Centre and improvement of the Market Place. The saddler's shop, owned by Mr. Grimes, was in business until 1956, when most of the growers were using tractors and lorries instead of horses for their work. Coulter's is now situated on the Four Pools Industrial Estate.

141 The workshop of Coulter's Garage in the 1920s.

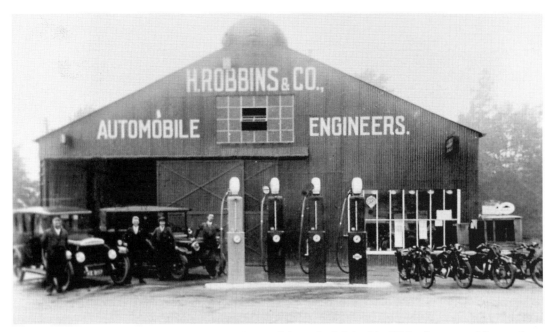

142 Tim Robbins, son of Harry Robbins and second from the left in this 1930s picture, was famous for his participation in motor cycle trials. He won many events and had gold medals, cups and other trophies to testify to his motor cycling skills.

143 0-6-0 freight engine No 1112 stands at the Midland Railway Station, Evesham.

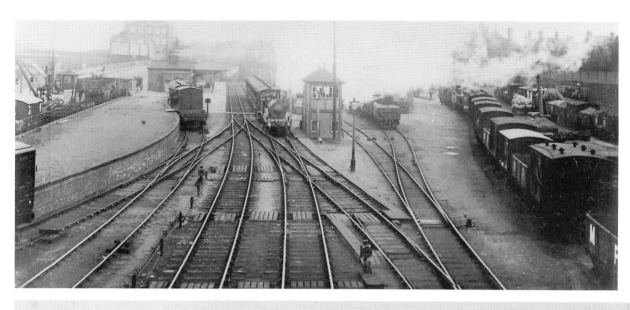

144 The Midland Railway Station and sidings (left) stand alongside the Great Western Railway Station at Evesham. This *c.*1906 view, looking east, shows the cramped site of the M.R. goods yard.

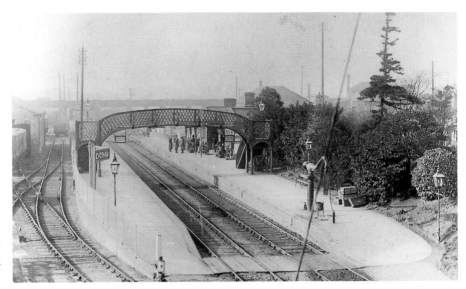

145 The Midland Railway Station, looking west, *c.*1906, with a train just leaving for Ashchurch.

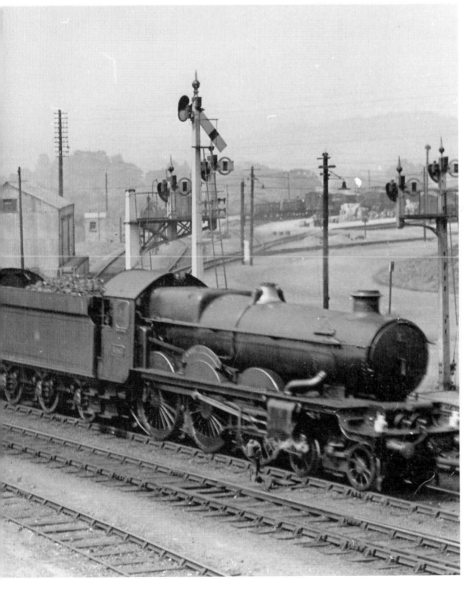

146 An unidentified 'Castle' class locomotive enters Evesham, with the 2 p.m. Worcester to Paddington express which carried Queen Mary from Ledbury to London on 31 July 1937. The Great Western Railway goods yard can be seen behind the engine.

147 The Great Western Railway Station at Evesham stood to the north of the later M.R. Station. Ex-G.W.R. 57xx class engine 4664 stands alongside the partly-demolished goods shed while taking on water on 11 November 1963.

Military

148 The Worcestershire Territorial Army band were photographed on the Almonry Green in 1897. Mr. G. Alcock, seated on the fifth chair from the drum, had a music shop in Evesham.

149 A group of local men, ready for the Boer War, were photographed in front of the porch of the old Evesham Grammar School on Merstow Green.

GUN WEEK AT EVESHA

150 Evesham Guns' Week, held during the last week of October 1918, was a successful attempt to raise £250,000 towards the war effort through the sale of National War Bonds. A howitzer, drawn by a small locomotive, was displayed in the High Street, along with a collection of war trophies which were displayed in the window of the Guns' Week Office. Every 15s. 6d. invested paid for 14lb. of high explosives, while a £5 bond would pay for a 5lb. shell. During the week, the howitzer also visited Badsey, the Littletons and Offenham.

National
War Bond

151 This now very rare sheet details the order of service for the Unveiling and Dedication of the Borough of Evesham War Memorial by the Vicar of Evesham on 7 August 1921.

152 Evesham War Memorial was unveiled on a site given by the Rudge family. The memorial is unusual in that 1920 is written on it as the date when war finished. This was because soldiers of the Worcestershire Regiment went to fight in Russia, where peace was not declared until 1920.

Back Row: J. A. Huxley, E. W. Dyer, S. C. S. Bedford, R. H. Emms, A. F. Sandalls, C. H. Davis, H. F. Brailsford, T. H. Emms, A. R. Staite, W. L. Badger, T. Major, G. D. L. Birch, G. T. Gisborne, B. L. Sheeham, A. J. Hands, R. F. Carter.

Middle Row: A. W. Gould, C. F. Cole, F. H. King, A. Wright, N. F. Grove, L/C. A. Plumb, W. G. Collings, L/C. A. G. Jones, L/C. E. W. Izod, L/C. F. Cleverley, Cpl. H. Hutchison, H. Workman, L. J. Andrews, W. Bailey, E. Townley, W. S. Dyde.

Front Row: Cpl. P. J. Mitchell, Cpl. W. H. Wootton, Sgt. G. Simpson, Sgt. G. Agar, Sgt. F. C. Ovard, C.S.M. H. Wood, M.M., Lieut. H. R. Smith, Lieut. J. A. Tate, Q.S.M. F. Edwards, Sgt. R. Wright, Sgt. J. H. Grinnell, Sgt. F. Darke, Cpl. T. W. Bailey, Cpl. J. Stanley.

Presented to Lieut. J. A. Tate by N.C.Os. and Men of No. 1 Platoon, February 17th, 1945

153 The No.1 Platoon, A Company of the 4th. Worcestershire (Evesham) Battalion of the Home Guard was led by Lieut. H. R. Smith (of the *Evesham Journal*) and Lieut. J. A. Tate (Latin master at Prince Henry's Grammar School). Several members of the platoon were also masters at the same school. The photograph was taken on the tennis courts of the school.

154 The Auxiliary Fire Service was stationed beneath the Town Hall during the Second World War. The town fire brigade remained in the building until a purpose-built fire station was erected on Merstow Green.

Education

155 In his will John Deacle, Alderman of the City of London, left enough money for the building of a school to educate 30 poor boys of Bengeworth. The school was built in 1736 at a cost of £335 and £2,000 was invested in land, the rent to be used for the upkeep of the school, the salary of the teacher, books, clothing and the eventual apprenticeship of the boys. After many successful years the school closed in 1906 and since then the premises have been put to various uses, including a Conservative & Unionist Club, a Labour Exchange and, at present, two shops.

156 This illustration of the original Abbey School porch displays the arms of Evesham Abbey with Clement Lichfield's initials and Tudor roses on the dripstone above the doorway.

ORATE PRO ANIMA CLEMENTIS ABBAT
1546

157 Prince Henry's Grammar School, *c.*1908. As well as the masters and the pupils, this school photograph even includes the gardener (on the left) and the school dog! The head master (centre, back row) was the Rev. St John Wilding. The pupils include Charles Field, Henry Fowler, Charles Fowler, Tom Byrd, Harry Averill, Bert Spiers and Henry Burlingham.

158 The children in this Merstow Green classroom sit up straight for the photographer, under the eagle eye of the master. The Merstow Green School was the first National School established in Fvesham.

159 Miss Hiden's class, Swan Lane, *c.*1930. The children are still in their socks as they have just risen from their afternoon nap.

160 Pupils and staff at Green Hill School, *c.*1930s.

Civics

161 Crowds gather in the Market Place for the declaration of the January 1906 Parliamentary election. Colonel Long polled 4,385 votes and his opponent Major Biggs 4,293, giving Colonel Long a majority of just ninety-two!

162 Sir Charles Cockerell was elected M.P. for Evesham many times during the first quarter of the 19th century. In 1818 there was a dispute about the validity of that year's election in which Sir Charles lost his seat to W. E. Rouse-Boughton. A petition was presented to Parliament in which Mr. Rouse-Boughton was accused of malpractice during the election. As a result of the petition and the ensuing investigation, Sir Charles was declared the duly elected Member of Parliament.

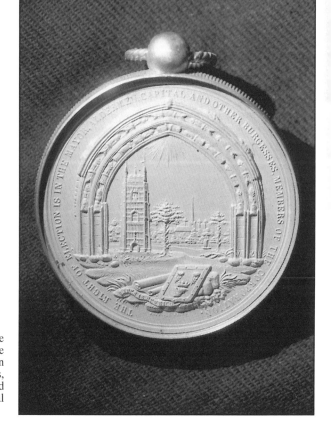

163 Sir Charles Cockerell had 400 commemorative medallions struck to celebrate his eventual victory in the 1818 election. Of these, 330 were bronze and were given to the burgesses of the borough and to his other supporters, while the remaining 70 were of silver and were intended for the principal inhabitants of the town and for his personal friends.

164 Evesham Borough Council. The Mayor and Mayoress are Councillor and Mrs. J. Hodges. Mrs. Amy Nightingale, wearing a tricorn hat, was elected as the first woman Mayor of Evesham, and possibly the Midlands, in 1944. She was the headmistress of the Evesham Council School in Swan Lane from 1919-40.

165 The Evesham Borough maces date from 1604, when they were given to the town by Sir Philip Keighley of South Littleton, who was Member of Parliament for Evesham at that time. These beautifully-crafted pieces of silver are held by Arthur Fryer, who is one of the town's mace-bearers. They are still used on all ceremonial occasions.

166 The Carew Cup and Plate were presented to the Evesham Corporation in 1660 by Alderman Carew of Aldington to commemorate the restoration of Charles II to the throne.

Personalities

167 When the Orleans family lived at Wood Norton they entertained many of their relatives and members of other European royal families. This 1904 portrait shows the Duc d'Orleans sitting third from the left. His sister, Queen Amelie of Portugal, third from the right, is seated next to him, with her husband, King Carlos, sitting beside her.

168 Wood Norton was once the home of the French Duc d'Orleans. The wedding of his sister, Princess Louise d'Orleans, and Prince Charles de Bourbon-Siciles took place here on 16 November 1907 and was attended by royalty from all over Europe. As the private chapel at Wood Norton was much too small for the ceremony, a large, wooden chapel was built at the side of the duc's residence. Painted to look like the stonework of the house, it was joined to the main building by a colonnade. Unfortunately the chapel had not been licensed for the solemnisation of matrimony, so early on the morning of the wedding the royal couple had to take their vows in a simple, official ceremony conducted in the corrugated iron hut which functioned as the Roman Catholic church in Evesham. The Orleans family left the estate in 1912. Today Wood Norton is a B.B.C. Training Centre.

169 The residents of Evesham took a keen interest in the activities of the Duc d'Orleans and his family. Crowds waited near Evesham Station hoping to see royalty arrive. Among the many distinguished guests were King Alfonso XIII of Spain, his wife, Queen Victoria Eugenie and Queen Amelie of Portugal. The Great Western Railway Company had decorated the station yard for the occasion and flags were also displayed throughout the town.

170 The royal wedding at Wood Norton was a spectacular occasion, the Duc d'Orleans having spent £30,000 on the arrangements. In this picture the wedding procession is passing through the graceful colonnade which linked the temporary chapel with the front door of the house.

The text on the bell reads:

CHURCH WARDENS 1821 REV. HENRY

SWEETLY TOLLING MEN DO CALL
TO TASTE ON FOOD THAT FEEDS THE SOUL

L. YEARS LATER
RECAST 1951 AND NAMED
CLEMENT LICHFIELD

THE LAW OF HIS GOD WAS IN HIS HEART

171 In 1951 the bells from the Bell Tower were recast. This view shows the vicar, Canon Jones, behind one of the bells. He was a well-known figure in the town, wearing his black hat and riding his tall bicycle. The gentleman on the right, wearing a light-coloured coat and holding a stick, was Mr. G. Hemming. He was ringing master in the Bell Tower and was a legend in his own lifetime. He taught many young bell ringers their art.

172 Through his publications George May contributed greatly to the preservation of the history of Evesham. Born in Bristol on 17 April 1803, he came to Evesham in 1828 at the age of 25 to take over the printing business of John Agg in Bridge Street. In 1834, on publishing a book about Evesham dedicated to his friends and fellow townsmen, 600 copies were sold. A second history appeared in 1845 entitled *Descriptive history of the town of Evesham*. May was particularly interested in religion and was associated with the dissenters' cause all his life. He died on 13 May 1871 and was buried in the graveyard of the Unitarian chapel in Oat Street.

173 George May's business was on the corner of Bridge Street and the Market Place. The building was later taken over by W. & H. Smith Ltd., who published the *Evesham Journal* and *Four Shires Advertiser*. The building is presently occupied by the national newsagents, W. H. Smith.

174 The distaff side and children of the Burlingham family were photographed in the 1890s. Sarah Burlingham is seated in the centre of the group with Edith Burlingham standing behind her.

175 The Bell Tower by Valentine Green, who was the son of a village dancing master. Believed to have been born in Salford Priors, he was certainly baptised there in 1739. He was apprenticed to William Phillips, Town Clerk of Evesham, to study law, but later joined what became the Worcester Porcelain Works. Here he was influenced by Robert Hancock, an engraver, and learnt the art of engraving on copper plates. In 1765 he went to London to study the art of mezzotint. Excelling in this field, he was elected to the Royal Academy. He was also an antiquary and historian, writing a history of Worcester, illustrated with his own engravings.

176 Henry Workman of Hampton was a local solicitor who became concerned about the state of the old Evesham Bridge after a woman was crushed to death by a passing waggon. Workman called a public meeting at the Town Hall at which a committee was formed to raise money to build a replacement. The town council gave £3,000 and the turnpike trusts put up £2,700 towards the cost of the bridge. Through Workman's exertion a further £3,500 was raised by public subscription. Henry Workman was elected mayor every year for the five years that it took to build the bridge. The new bridge was named after him. He was also responsible for the construction of the Workman Pleasure Grounds on Waterside just below the bridge and which were also named after him.

177 A portrait of the New family. The bearded Herbert New was Mayor of Evesham from 1919 to 1920. He was made an honorary Freeman of the Borough in 1928. The casket, with its miniature scenes of Evesham, and the scroll which were presented to him, can be seen in the Almonry Museum. His son Edward Hort New, the artist and illustrator, is the young man holding a tennis racquet with his right hand.

178 Edmund Hort New was born in Evesham on 6 December 1871. He was educated at Prince Henry's Grammar School and the Birmingham School of Art, studying under E. R. Taylor and A. J. Gaskin. Famous for the New Loggan Series of plates of the Oxford colleges, he also illustrated *The Compleat Angler* and *The Natural History of Selborne*. He wrote and illustrated a book on Evesham, too. His kindness, extreme thoughtfulness and consideration for others gained him many friends. New died on 3 February 1931. This drawing of the Walker Hall by New is typical of his work, of which there is a very good collection in the town's Almonry Museum.

179 Ettwell Augustine Barnard was born in Evesham, at the High Street's Worcester City & County Bank, which is now Lloyds Bank. After attending Prince Henry's Grammar School, he went to Italy and Sicily to study history and archaeology. Writing copiously for the *Evesham Journal*, Barnard's articles were very popular. The author of books on local history, such as *Tower and bells of Evesham* and *Story of Dresden House*, he assisted the Rev. J. P. Shawcross with a book on Bengeworth, which was published in 1927. Barnard took an active part in the social life of Evesham, serving on numerous committees and playing important roles in the Operatic Society productions, besides being a governor of Prince Henry's Grammar School and secretary of the Bell Tower Restoration Fund. In 1951 he was the fourth person to become an Honorary Freeman of the Borough of Evesham. He is seen here (standing) during the ceremony.

180 The first library in Evesham was built in the Market Place in 1824. The building was enlarged in 1862 with the addition of reading rooms and classrooms for adult education. It became known as the Evesham Literary, Scientific and Mechanics' Institute. The library remained in this building, in cramped conditions, until it moved to the Public Hall in 1909. In May 1975 part of the library moved to the nearby Walker Hall, the remainder staying in the Public Hall until 1989, when redevelopment forced it to move to the Town Hall. Finally, the library moved to new premises, opened by H.R.H. the Princess Margaret, in Oat Street in 1990.

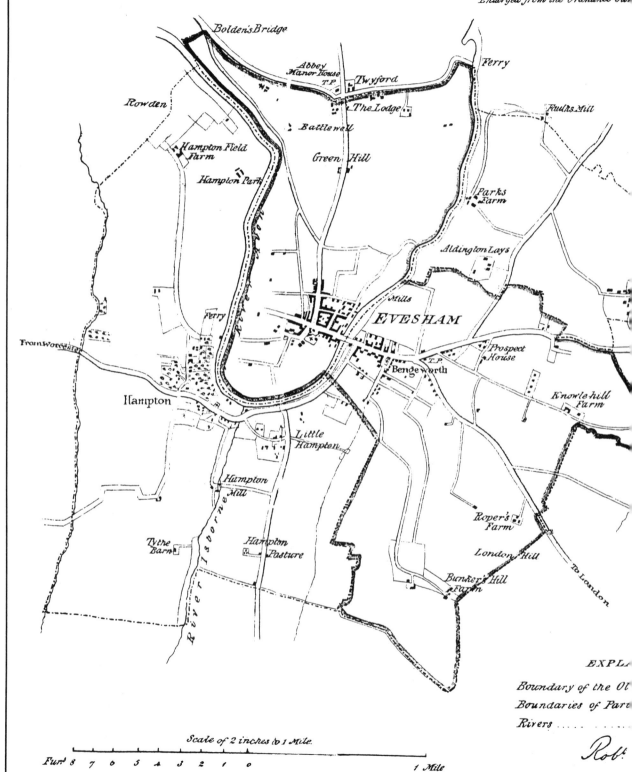

EVESHAM

Enlarged from the Ordnance Sur

Bolden's Bridge

Rowden

Abbey
Manor House
T.P.

Ferry

Twyford

The Lodge

Faulks Mill

Hampton Field
Farm

Battle well

Green Hill

Parks
Farm

Hampton Park

Aldington Lays

Ferry

Mills

EVESHAM

FromWorcester

Prospect
House

Bengeworth

T.P.

Hampton

Knowle hill
Farm

Little
Hampton

Hampton
Mill

River Isborne

Roper's
Farm

London Hill

To London

Tythe
Barn

Hampton
Pasture

Bunker's Hill
Farm

EXPLA

Boundary of the Ol

Boundaries of Part

Rivers . . . .

Scale of 2 inches to 1 Mile.

Fur.⁸ 8 7 6 5 4 3 2 1 0

1 Mile

Rob.